BRACHIOSAURUS

by Laura K. Murray

Consultant: Mathew J. Wedel, PhD
Western University of Health Sciences
Pomona, California

PEBBLE
a capstone imprint

Published by Pebble, an imprint of Capstone
1710 Roe Crest Drive, North Mankato, Minnesota 56003
capstonepub.com

Copyright © 2026 by Capstone. All rights reserved. No part of this publication may be reproduced in whole or in part, or stored in a retrieval system, or transmitted in any form or by any means, electronic, mechanical, photocopying, recording, or otherwise, without written permission of the publisher.

Library of Congress Cataloging-in-Publication Data is available on the Library of Congress website.

ISBN: 9798875226793 (hardcover)
ISBN: 9798875234057 (paperback)
ISBN: 9798875234064 (ebook PDF)

Summary: Describes Brachiosaurus, where it lived, what it ate, how it behaved, how it was discovered, and more.

Editorial Credits
Designer: Dina Her; Media Researcher: Jo Miller; Production Specialist: Tori Abraham

Image Credits
Alamy: Photo12/7e Art/Universal Pictures 28; Capstone: Jon Hughes, 5, 6, 9, 14, 17; Getty Images: iStock/ALLVISIONN, 24, iStock/dottedhippo, 12, 25, MARK GARLICK/SCIENCE PHOTO LIBRARY, 1, 8, 11, 20, ROGER HARRIS/SCIENCE PHOTO LIBRARY, 19; Science Source: Millard H. Sharp, 27; Shutterstock: Alberto Andrei Rosu, cover, Chris Curtis, 22, Dmitry Porotnikov, 21, Kues (background), cover and throughout, Nisansala99, 16; Superstock: Ingo Schulz/imageBROKER, 15

Any additional websites and resources referenced in this book are not maintained, authorized, or sponsored by Capstone. All product and company names are trademarks™ or registered® trademarks of their respective holders.

Table of Contents

Long-Necked Dinosaur 4

Where in the World 7

Brachiosaurus Bodies 10

What Brachiosaurus Ate 16

Life of Brachiosaurus 20

Discovering Brachiosaurus 22

    Fast Facts 29

    Glossary 30

    Read More 31

    Internet Sites 31

    Index 32

    About the Author 32

Words in **bold** are in the glossary.

Long-Necked Dinosaur

What plant-eating dinosaur had a long neck? Brachiosaurus! Its name means "arm lizard." The name comes from its front legs, or "arms." Its front legs were longer than its back legs. It had a long neck like a giraffe.

Brachiosaurus lived during the Late Jurassic Period. That was about 155 million to 140 million years ago.

Where in the World

Brachiosaurus lived in what is now the western United States. Scientists have found **fossils** in Colorado, Oklahoma, Utah, and Wyoming.

When Brachiosaurus lived, the western United States had more flat land. There were rivers, lakes, and streams. There were wet seasons and dry seasons. It was warmer than today.

Ferns and very old kinds of trees grew everywhere. Grasses and flowers did not exist yet. Many dinosaurs lived on the land. **Mammals** were the size of mice, rats, and badgers. Snails, fish, and turtles lived in the water. There were creatures like crocodiles too.

Brachiosaurus stayed on flat land. It likely did not climb or run. It moved slowly. It was a lot of work to move its big body.

Brachiosaurus Bodies

Brachiosaurus is part of a group of big dinosaurs. They were plant-eaters with long necks and tails. They had four legs. Other dinosaurs in the group include Apatosaurus.

Brachiosaurus grew to 40 to 50 feet (12 to 16 meters) tall. That is as tall as a four-story building! Brachiosaurus was more than 80 feet (24 m) long. It may have weighed more than 99,000 pounds (44,906 kg).

Did You Know?

Brachiosaurus is one of the biggest animals ever to have lived on Earth.

Brachiosaurus had a small head. Its long neck had a curve like the letter S. Its legs were thick and strong. Its long front legs made it extra tall. It had a thick, powerful tail.

Brachiosaurus's heart was large and strong. It pumped blood through the dinosaur's big body.

Brachiosaurus had **nostrils** near the front of its snout. They led to large nose holes on top of its skull. Scientists think this may have kept the dinosaur's brain cool.

Brachiosaurus skull

Inside the Brachiosaurus jaw were 52 teeth. They were shaped like spoons. The teeth could snip off lots of plants at once. Brachiosaurus didn't chew before it swallowed.

What Brachiosaurus Ate

Brachiosaurus ate different kinds of plants. It ate trees called conifers. Conifers have cones. Their leaves look like needles or scales. Brachiosaurus likely ate gingko leaves and ferns too. It also ate palm-like plants called cycads.

cycad

Brachiosaurus needed a lot of food for its large body. It ate up to 880 pounds (399 kg) of food each day!

Brachiosaurus could get plants from high places. It likely did not stand up on its back legs. It just stretched its long neck.

The size of Brachiosaurus was helpful in other ways too. The plants it ate were hard to **digest**. A big body could break down food better. Brachiosaurus could stand in one place. Then it could eat a ton of food!

Life of Brachiosaurus

Brachiosaurus hatched from an egg. Bigger **predators** might try to eat a baby dinosaur. But Brachiosaurus grew fast. It may have grown up to 30 pounds (14 kg) a day. An adult Brachiosaurus did not have predators. Other animals did not want to fight it. It was too big.

Brachiosaurus may have used its long neck in different ways. It may have helped show how strong it was to other dinosaurs. It may have helped in showing off to **mates**.

Discovering Brachiosaurus

In 1900, scientist Elmer Riggs was working in western Colorado. It was part of the large area called the Morrison Formation. Riggs found part of a dinosaur skeleton. He named it Brachiosaurus in 1903.

Morrison Formation

This skeleton helped people learn about other fossils. In 1883, scientist Othniel Marsh had found a dinosaur skull in Colorado. People thought it was an Apatosaurus. But it was really a Brachiosaurus.

Did You Know?
Scientists used horses to help pull the Brachiosaurus bone out of the Morrison Formation.

People used to think Brachiosaurus lived in water. But then they learned more. They changed their minds. Scientists now think that Brachiosaurus lived on land.

For a long time, scientists thought Brachiosaurus was the biggest dinosaur ever. But new dinosaurs were found. They were likely much bigger.

People have found very few Brachiosaurus fossils. In 2009, scientists found out some Brachiosaurus fossils were not Brachiosaurus after all. They were different dinosaurs!

In 2019, scientists made an exciting find. They found a fossil in the Morrison Formation in Utah. It was the leg bone of Brachiosaurus. It weighed almost 1,000 pounds (454 kg).

Brachiosaurus skull fossil

Brachiosaurus is a popular dinosaur. It shows up in books, movies, and art. Chicago has a famous model of a Brachiosaurus skeleton. It is at the O'Hare International Airport.

Today scientists study fossils of Brachiosaurus. They have many questions. There is still a lot to learn about this amazing, long-necked dinosaur!

Did You Know?
Brachiosaurus appeared in the movie *Jurassic World: Fallen Kingdom*.

Fast Facts

Name: Brachiosaurus (meaning "arm lizard")

Lived: Late Jurassic (155 million to 140 million years ago)

Range: western United States

Habitat: flat floodplains

Food: plants such as conifers, cycads, and gingkoes

Threats: none

Discovered: 1900, Colorado

Glossary

digest (die-JEST)—to break down food in the stomach

fossil (FA-suhl)—the remains or traces of a living thing from many years ago

mammal (MAM-uhl)—a warm-blooded animal that has hair or fur; usually gives birth to live young

mate (MAYT)—a partner that joins with another to produce young

nostril (NAWS-tril)—outer opening of the nose used for breathing

predator (PRED-uh-tur)—an animal that hunts other animals for food

Read More

Gregory, Josh. *Discover the Brachiosaurus.* Ann Arbor, MI: Cherry Lake Publishing, 2025.

Greve, Meg. *Super-Incredible Dinosaurs.* Mankato, MN: Black Rabbit Books, 2025.

Vonder Brink, Tracy. *The Brachiosaurus.* New York: Crabtree Publishing, 2024.

Internet Sites

Enchanted Learning: Brachiosaurus
enchantedlearning.com/subjects/dinosaurs/dinos/Brachiosaurus.shtml

National Geographic Kids: Brachiosaurus
kids.nationalgeographic.com/animals/prehistoric/facts/brachiosaurus

Natural History Museum: Brachiosaurus
nhm.ac.uk/discover/dino-directory/brachiosaurus.html

Index

discovery, 22, 23, 26, 29

eggs, 20

food, 15, 16, 17, 18, 29
fossils, 7, 23, 26, 28

legs, 4, 13, 18, 26

mates, 21

name, 4, 22, 29
neck, 4, 10, 13, 18, 21, 28
nostrils, 14

predators, 20

size, 10, 11, 13, 17, 18, 20, 24

tail, 10, 13
teeth, 15

when it lived, 4, 7, 29
where it lived, 7, 8, 9, 24, 29

About the Author

Laura K. Murray is the Minnesota-based author of more than 100 books for young readers. She loves learning from fellow readers and helping others find their reading superpowers! Visit LauraKMurray.com.